For God's Sake
Pay Attention

For God's Sake Pay Attention

Realizing Life While We Live It
Poems and Reflections about the Journey

JODY SEYMOUR

RESOURCE *Publications* • Eugene, Oregon

FOR GOD'S SAKE PAY ATTENTION
Realizing Life While We Live It: Poems and Reflections about the Journey

Copyright © 2025 Jody Seymour. All rights reserved. Except for brief quotations in critical publications or reviews, no part of this book may be reproduced in any manner without prior written permission from the publisher. Write: Permissions, Wipf and Stock Publishers, 199 W. 8th Ave., Suite 3, Eugene, OR 97401.

Resource Publications
An Imprint of Wipf and Stock Publishers
199 W. 8th Ave., Suite 3
Eugene, OR 97401

www.wipfandstock.com

PAPERBACK ISBN: 979-8-3852-4644-1
HARDCOVER ISBN: 979-8-3852-4645-8
EBOOK ISBN: 979-8-3852-4646-5

04/28/25

I am grateful for Gail Spach's careful editing of this book. I may have insight as a poet but lack detail when it comes to proofreading, so thank you, Gail.

I am also indebted to my friend Shawn, who in many early morning hours listened attentively to my reading of a lot of these poems and responded with care and appreciation.

"The reason I speak to them in parables is that 'seeing they do not perceive, and hearing they do not listen, nor do they understand.' With them indeed is fulfilled the prophecy of Isaiah that says: '... For this people's heart has grown dull, and their ears are hard of hearing, and they have shut their eyes; so that they might not look with their eyes, and listen with their ears, and understand with their heart and turn—and I would heal them.'"

MATTHEW 13:13–15 (NRSV)

"When the Buddha started to wander around India shortly after his enlightenment, he encountered several men who recognized him to be a very extraordinary being. They asked him: "Are you a god?" "No," he replied. "Are you a reincarnation of god?" "No," he replied. "Are you a wizard, then?" "No." "Well, are you a man?" "No." "So what are you?" they asked, being very perplexed. Buddha simply replied: "I am awake."

BUDDHIST TEACHING

"The sixteen of us who traveled together were ... lovers who ... decided to make the world a better place by slowing down long enough to pay for its improvement—by paying attention, the reverent, even holy attention of love."

BRIAN MCLAREN, *THE GALAPAGOS ISLANDS: A SPIRITUAL JOURNEY*

EMILY: "Does anyone ever realize life while they live it ... every, every minute?"
STAGE MANAGER: "No. Saints and poets maybe ... they do some."

THORNTON WILDER, *OUR TOWN*

Instructions for living a life:
Pay attention.
Be astonished.
Tell about it.

MARY OLIVER, FROM THE POEM "SOMETIMES," IN *RED BIRD*

Contents

So Why? | xiii
A Suggestion | xv

THE NATURAL WORLD | 1

Creation Waits | 3
Ask the Breeze | 5
The Gift of Small Things | 7
Breath's Gift | 9
Seasons | 11
Into Darkness Light | 13
Deep in the Heart | 15
Leaf Thoughts | 18
An Orchestra of Love | 20

LIFE AND FAITH | 23

Hope's Dream | 25
From Where Tenderness | 28
The Peace I Seek | 30
Take Time | 32
Into the Questions | 35
Seeds of Hope | 37
Loneliness Bids Welcome | 39
Past Present Future | 41

CONTENTS

Inside Out | 45
Today Is All We Have | 48
What Matters? | 50
Tears of the Heart . . . Flowers of Hope | 52
The Second Chance | 54
The Journey | 56
Wounded Soul | 58
God's Fatigue | 60
There Is a Place of Deep Peace | 62
Adrift Yet Afloat | 64
Where Is My End? | 66
Welcome O Wanderer | 68
To Begin Again | 70
In This Moment | 72
No Open Doors | 74

THEMES FROM SCRIPTURE | 77

The Lost Garden | 80
Still Waiting | 82
Deep the Valley | 84
There You Are | 87
Fear Not | 89
Waters of Grace | 91
Waiting on God | 93
A Young Jesus Ponders His Two Fathers | 95
A Large Man with Small Thoughts | 98
No Way | 100
Where Can I Find You? | 104
Lonely Wait | 106
Forever Thirsty | 109
Foolish Love | 112
And Now | 114

Where Are the Nine? | 116
Free as I Long to Be | 118
Calm My Storm | 120
Grace too Late? | 122
Blurred Vision | 125
So Lost but Found | 127

ADVENT AND CHRISTMAS | 131

It Can't Be | 134
Destined to Fly | 136
Which Wilderness? | 138
Pregnant Pause | 140
Into the Longing | 142
In Need of Filling | 144
Seeking Joy | 146
His Eyes See Me | 148
Limping Toward a Manger | 150
No Surprise | 153
Is It Too Full? | 154
It's About Time | 156
Mary Pondered | 158
Sleep Bethlehem | 161
What If? | 164
Listen to the Quiet | 166
Who Needs Christmas? | 168

LENT AND EASTER | 171

Light's Journey | 175
On His Knees | 177
My Heart Reaches Out | 179
What Kind of Love? | 182
Finally or Not | 184

Contents

Lonely Grace | 187
Pietà | 189
Everything Waits | 191
There Is a Way | 193
Death's Lament | 195
Dark for Three Days | 198
Running Toward Resurrection | 200
Feeding Time | 202

A LAST THOUGHT | 205

A Tribute to Jimmy Buffet | 205
A Pirate's Paradise | 206

So Why?

So why do I share these words with you? The haunting lines in the introductory quotes from the play *Our Town* have stayed with me over the years: does anyone actually ever realize life while they live it?

In my "advanced age," I discovered the need for cataract surgery. Others shared with me how different my vision would be after the surgery, how much brighter and clearer the world would be. They were right. But what I realized is that we also develop spiritual cataracts. Our vision becomes dull over the years, and we miss so much of what is before us.

In the play, Emily is given the opportunity after her untimely death to witness a single day in her life. It is her twelfth birthday, and she is astounded to see that the people she knows so well, but who cannot see her, are simply not paying attention to life. The words she speaks remain as a caution and an invitation to us all. The other quotes I have shared point to the same deep truth. We become accustomed to a dimmed vision of life without realizing it. Dull becomes normal.

Jesus told those who would listen that a danger people face is seeing but not perceiving, and hearing but not listening nor understanding. Then he made it his mission to heal their hearing and, well, surgically remove their spiritual cataracts. I have often told people that if you distill Jesus' wisdom teachings into one phrase it would be, "For God's sake, pay attention!" Before Emily's words resonated with me, I suppose it was Jesus who first got my attention, and so I share this book.

So Why?

Another wisdom teacher quoted above told those who inquired that he was neither a wizard nor a god but simply "awake." How often do we sleepwalk through life and not "realize it?" Then, Brian McLaren calls us to slow down and love life rather than treating existence as if it is some kind of commodity that we have purchased. One of my other book titles sums up the whole matter: "Lost but Making Excellent Time."

So why do I share these poems and reflections with you? I found that I needed my spiritual cataracts removed. I discovered that life is not a rehearsal for a later performance. Poetry is the language of the soul, so I share these poems with you as a way to encourage you to slow down and pay attention. The poems reflect themes from Scripture, issues of life and faith, and the natural world. I also include poems focusing on two of the seasons of faith: Lent and Easter and Advent and Christmas. Those two seasons are times when Christian pilgrims are especially called to slow down and pay attention.

Children are taught at an early age to stop, look, and listen. Jesus told those who would hear that anyone who wished to understand and gain entrance to the new kingdom he offered must "come as a child." In the busy and often crazy adult world, the child in each of us needs to stop, look, and listen so that we might see and hear the Divine in our midst. I offer these words from that place in me where the child lives, as signposts along the way. I hope they speak to the child in you that longs for notice.

The Stage Manager answers Emily's plaintive question by saying that saints and poets may be the only ones paying attention to life while it is being lived and even then, only some of them. Saints are simply those pilgrims who pay attention and aim to help God heal the world—and—poets? Well, we all have a language of the soul; we can all be poets. I invite you to journey with me as we pay attention and realize life while living it.

A Suggestion

"Life can be a poem instead of a trail."

Richard Rohr

As you read the poems in this book, you may of course read them as you wish, but I offer the following suggestion for your consideration. Richard Rohr also offers this counsel about how to observe life: "First of all, there is the seeing, and then there is the recognizing; the second stage is called contemplation."

If you wish to contemplate the poems, one way to do that is as follows:

- Read the poem slowly.
- Read it again noticing a word or phrase that stands out to you.
- Finally, ponder why that word or phrase spoke to you and what it might mean in your journey.

The Natural World

CREATION IS CONSTANTLY ASKING us to pay attention, but we so often walk on by. Perhaps burning bushes are more ubiquitous than we expect, but in our haste to arrive somewhere, we fail to take off our shoes.

St. Francis realized after his conversion to a new way of seeing, hearing, and thinking that he was kin to all creation. His family included Brother Sun, Sister Moon, and Mother Earth. Tradition has it that the birds waited for Francis to expound the truth of creation to them:

> "My brother and sister birds, you should praise your Creator and always love him: He gave you feathers for clothes, wings to fly and all other things that you need. It is God who made you noble among all creatures, making your home in the air. Without sowing or reaping, you receive God's guidance and protection."

Jesus used creation to invite those who would pay attention not to worry so much. He told anxiety-ridden disciples that the birds of the air and the flowers of the field appeared to be free from the bondage of despairing about the future. God's care for the birds and the flowers was a reminder that his followers were worth more than their worry.

Jesus loved to use the elements of creation to tell his stories. Seeds became symbols of a kingdom that was amid everyday events. The wheat and the tares in the parable in Matthew 13:24–30 were portrayals of the inability of small-minded people to truly judge reality and a caution that only the owner of the field was the true judge.

Before St. Francis claimed kinship with creation, Jesus proved that he was ruler of wind and wave. Fig trees became symbols of faith and faithlessness. The sacred story contained in the Scriptures begins with a garden and ends with a river that flows by the throne of the Creator. All creation is an icon of God's effort to wake up those who will observe the wonder of all that is.

What follows are poems that reflect our constant need to be attentive to the visual miracles that happen daily if we will but notice. You will discover in these ponderings the chance to wait upon creation. You will be offered the opportunity to "ask the breeze." The "gift of small" will be made real for those who think that only the spectacular is important.

The treasure of our breath will be measured in words. The changing seasons will be celebrated as they move both within and through us. The reality of darkness will be valued and its lessons noted. The long ago act of creation will reveal a heart at the center of it all. Cosmic music will be heard as an "orchestra of love." And the thoughts of a solitary leaf will be heard as a form of natural wisdom.

Creation always waits for us to "pay attention—for God's sake."

CREATION WAITS

Before time was time
God waited amidst a pause
that would create eternity
In no hurry was the
divine worker of wonder

Worlds were but thoughts
before that instant
when light would shatter
the darkness of chaos

No random accident
are we who now ponder
Creation's gift given
without the asking
Behold echoes the voice
of one who thought
it all up in a moment
called *In the beginning*

Look into the night sky or
hold a flower in your grasp
Forget for a time the
rapid pace of your life
Hold back the new chaos
of yesterday's lost hopes
or the future's worry

Now is the moment of grace
Creation waited
in a time long ago
And now Creation waits on you

ASK THE BREEZE

Why am I even here?
The question seemed to
linger beside my
desire to know

We are living questions
souls longing to fill
the gaps of mystery

Not hearing an answer
we busy our time
with constant motion
forgetting to even
ask about the meaning
of our lives
lived so fast

So now pause—ask
the breeze
as it moves the leaves
of your tree of life
And as you ponder the
movement of wonder
you may hear an answer

*You are filled with the
breeze of life
Your first breath
was given to you
by the maker of the breeze
You are a miracle
though you so often
forget the source of it all*

Ask the breeze . . .
Listen . . .
and whisper in
its direction,
Thank you

THE GIFT OF SMALL THINGS

The window of my world
is large and so I
see a scene of moments
of time that move quickly
and without form

Then comes a strange awakening
Pay attention to
the small things
Wondering the meaning
of words from afar
I see the ridges on my fingers
as if for the first time

As I walk outside my window
barefoot for some unknown reason
I feel the edges of the
grass as if to
make me pause and ponder
the carpet upon which
I have walked
numb so many times

The cricket's song this time
noticed calls to me
and leads me toward a blossom
on a tree that awaits my vision
How many times has it stood
alone in its beauty?

Then comes the breath
Many are they each day
life offered without request
filling me with moments
so forgotten because
I notice not small things

I close my eyes and my
soul smiles at this
reminder from a place
of waiting wonder
Notice the small things
and life will become large

BREATH'S GIFT

Without notice they come
as gifts neglected
full of consuming thoughts
we hurriedly travel
to whatever is next

What if some mystical stranger
comes from behind
and taps us on
the shoulder asking,
How many came your way?

Confused by the question
we pause and
wonder why was
such an inquiry necessary
Our lives are full
of no time for
such mystery

Then our tired spirit
reaches into some
deep cavern to seek
the stranger's meaning

In the silence comes the
same question with
a completion so needed
*How many breaths
have been given
you?*

Breaths . . . given?
Were they not of
our own making?
And in the questioning pause
comes the answer
*Each breath was
a gift forgotten
filling you with life
that comes from
beyond your reach*

So now take in
the next gift
and whisper
under your breath,
Thank you

SEASONS

Around me change speaks
truth for my hearing
Within you are seasons

Winter's cold whisper
bids me pause
to remember the
waiting time when
life seems barren
and warmth comes slowly
to my expectant
heart

Beyond my questioning horizon
there is a spring not yet
ripe for my picking
I sense a kind of
cosmic tease that
entices my imagination
and gives me hope
that nature's promise
is also
for me

Summer's warm breezes
are now still and
wait beneath my
anxious thoughts about
an unknown future
But a divine smile greets
my impatience reminding me
Not yet

The autumn of my longing
will color hopes and dreams
but in this moment I must
believe in promises
felt even now in the
chill of not knowing

Winter's blanket surrounds
me and I rest in
the deep assurance that
within me are seasons
In my waiting I remember
that I am part of
all that is
and I say *thank you*
for all my seasons

INTO DARKNESS LIGHT

(A poem about the dawn of Creation)

Into darkness there came
a presence seeking to
fill a waiting void
A power beyond imagining
created Creation
Its light desired form
to be later seen
by souls needing
to know there
was more than
veiled emptiness

So everything that came to be
filled all space
and time
The sound of it can
be heard in the
one who quiets
their busy spirit
and listens to the
beating of
the life within

Into darkness light
The reach of Creation
can again fill your
vacant places
From the beginning
a soul of love
longed to be present
to all deep questions

Never are you alone
comes the echo
of a Creator's resounding
beginning that
happened so that
you may always know
that no matter how
deep the darkness
there will be
light

*The light shines in
the darkness and the
darkness did not
overcome it*

DEEP IN THE HEART

Deep in the heart of
all that is
a birth waited
to be
Its life was long
in coming
and until its arrival
there was emptiness

The darkness of longing
felt surprise as
it encountered this
new encompassing
light that seemed
to fill all the places
of waiting need

Creation breathed a
long and lasting
new breath
The wind suddenly
felt a fullness
that was not
present before

Deep in the heart of
all that is
Love came into being
It is and was
always meant
to be the reason
for everything

Pause in this moment
and know
You are the result of
Love's birth
No blind thought brought
you into reality

You are *Love's* child
bound to what
was created in
the beginnings of
long ago

You are filled with
Love's need to
touch everything
that lives and breathes

Rest in this moment
and feel
who you really are . . .
Reach in
Reach out
and receive
your reason
to be . . .
Love

LEAF THOUGHTS

Waiting on a journey that
will take me away
from the holding on
that was long in coming
Much have I seen as
growth offered me
glimpses of a world
full of wonder

So many pass by without
notice of what
seems to be ordinary
Missing is the vision
to see beauty
in the making

My source often weeps
at their blind
busyness amidst a
world that spins too fast
to notice the
ever present miracle

Soon I will give way to
the old necessity of
a change that is
meant to be
But in my fall there
is a soon to be
revealing of new growth
waiting for someone
to notice the marvel
of it all

AN ORCHESTRA OF LOVE

Could it be that all
that came to be
was an orchestra of love
The cosmic conductor
dreamed up a new
melody birthed
from deep within
a place of utter joy

Not being able to contain
the thought of what
a creation might sound like
chords stirred anew
like the bubbling of
some underground spring

Suddenly light crashed
upon the scene
in a crescendo of
what seemed like
glee from a child
at play

Then came the murmur of
a bird's song to
accompany the still
silence that awaited
its coming

Someone needs to hear
this music
thought the conductor
So in this moment
close your eyes
and listen with care
to the wonder . . .
It's all for you

Life and Faith

> "To journey without being changed is to be a nomad. To change without journeying is to be a chameleon. To journey and to be transformed by the journey is to be a pilgrim."
>
> MARK NEPO, *THE BOOK OF AWAKENING: HAVING THE LIFE YOU WANT BY BEING PRESENT IN THE LIFE YOU HAVE*

WE CAN TRAVEL THROUGH life acting like tourists who are visiting the sights, or we can do as Mark Nepo suggests, journey through life as a pilgrim who notices what is happening. Paying attention to the journey has transformative powers.

One way to travel our road of life is with an attitude like the protagonist of Lewis Carroll's *Alice in Wonderland*:

> Alice: Would you tell me, please, which way I ought to go from here?
> The Cheshire Cat: That depends a good deal on where you want to get to.
> Alice: I don't much care where.
> The Cheshire Cat: Then it doesn't much matter which way you go.
> Alice: . . . So long as I get somewhere.
> The Cheshire Cat: Oh, you're sure to do that, if only you walk long enough.

The spiritual journey is not about "walking long enough"—it is about realizing life while we live it. Jesus longed for those around him who have eyes to see to really see. In the movie *Avatar*, the

Na'vi people use the phrase "Oel ngati kame," which means "I see you." This expression conveys not just the perception of a person but an insight into the person. It means, "I am paying attention to you. I hear you. I want to know who you really are, not just what you look like. I understand you." This is what Jesus is talking about when he desires for those who follow him to see life as gift, to see others as people on a journey with you.

The poems that follow are offered as a way to see issues of faith and life. The words deal with hope, peace, time, tenderness, tears, and other signposts that appear on our journey as we pay attention. My hope is that as you read these words, they will not be just sights along the trip but insights for your pilgrimage.

HOPE'S DREAM

I rest beside despair
seeking a time to
shed my light into
the dark recess
of questions whose
answers seem empty
I am *Hope* and
my name is echoed
in times past
when the soul's
sense of reason
appeared to have
no peace to offer
your restless spirit

I know your name
and I am the friend
you thought lost
to life's constant
cry of futility
that is often not
as real as your
dim vision
thinks so

Feel the beat of my
full heart that is
as close as your
next breath
I always wait to
arise as the sun
for the dawning
of hope when
you think there
is none to have

So in this moment close
your eyes and know
I am there
My knowing of you
is deep with
a love that will
not leave when
doubt wishes to
take you away
from me

I am *Hope* and
I am present in
moments when life
seems to unravel
and tear
It is then that
my healing is
meant for you

Lean into me and
know I am
Hope

FROM WHERE TENDERNESS

The longing of all is
tenderness's gift
Its warmth melts the
rigid shell surrounding
the hard heart

Its seed was planted in
a time of unknowing
when the distant yet close
heartbeat of a mother
offered the sound
of a mysterious welcome

But soon a distance was
felt in a world of
new places to wander away
from the close encounter
of love's invitation to
share tenderness's gift

Surrounded are we by
souls longing for
the soon-forgotten gift
of a filling so wanted
by that past sound
of the womb's caress of
accepting love

So seek the opening in life's
often closed places
and offer a word . . . a touch . . .
a not-so-silent look
of wanting to know
the story of the pilgrim
whose road you share

If we all do the same then
our hungry world
filled with busy but
lonely seekers
will feel the gift
so needed by all . . .
tenderness

THE PEACE I SEEK

Restless is my wondering
spirit that seeks
answers to questions
that seem beyond
the limits of
my reach

From where does this
continual longing come?
Wanting to be filled
like an empty cup
I seek for a peace
that is deeper
than the instant
pleasures my hunger
seems to want

I peer into a future that
my anxious thoughts
long to control
only to discover a
door whose latch
is on the other side
I stand looking toward
a winding road
and then the wind

speaks to me
in words that must
come from a place
of mystery
The peace you seek is within
buried beneath
your limited vision

Look inside and
discover a
calm place that
waits for you
Peace is a gift
beyond your
tiring efforts
Receive it

TAKE TIME

I was before you
and will be after
what you have
is over
Waiting for your
first breath
I paused to notice
your importance

Some think of me as
mystery because I
cannot be possessed
but only held
gently as a gift
called *the present*

I witness all your days
while mostly going
unnoticed and lost
amidst the swirl
of a pace too
hurried for any
peace to be birthed

I am *Time* and my
presence is always
there for your taking
Each breath is my
quiet messenger
In this pondering moment
as I gain your attention
what do you hear
me say?

My gifts come not in
large portions
to be consumed
by an all too hungry soul
Small is my nature and
silent is my voice
heard only between
the noise of haste

Just now
I hold you
I smile at your
tiring efforts to
measure me
Rest in the reality
that each moment
of mine is precious
and remember
A thousand years in
my sight
are but as yesterday
when it is past

Take time to
notice

INTO THE QUESTIONS

Like a child seeking
answers to quiet
mysteries that appear
from a place of
wonder
we long to know

The longing is at times
a presence that becomes
a blanket of
needed warmth
but then can be
a capturing net

So the child in us
no matter the number
of our years
yearns to ask deep
questions often beginning
with *Why*
Then we wait as if
some messenger will
appear at the doorway
of our soul
to deliver a long-awaited
answer

Such waiting wastes precious
moments that slip by
like a dew that is
but a fleeting promise
The present moment
seeks an embrace
missed because
attention is lost
to a seeking
without end

Rest now with your questions
Some answers are for
a later time when
the morning mist of
life's gift will clear
Then will come a dawning
that will reveal
that we now stand on
the other side of a
mirror dim

All will be well
That is the promise
from the other side
of our Whys
Trust the promise
Live the questions

SEEDS OF HOPE

Scattered by some wind
that seems to blow
from the edge of grace
they fall upon our
places of waiting
seeds of hope

Not earned by any
effort of will
they simply are
Their source matters not
Our dry spirits are
tired from a journey
in need of a place
of rest and surprise

In this moment notice
their small presence
They come in the
arid times when
our dry spirits
long simply to see
what might be
new beginnings

Seeds of hope
Allow them to be
planted in your
field of life so
often cluttered with
weeds of wrong choices

Hope's small flowers
can grow large
for those who will
see that a power
from beyond
really cares
Seeds of hope

LONELINESS BIDS WELCOME

The quiet vacancy waits
for a filling that
fails to come
Expectant hopes lie
broken beside tired feet
that long to rest
from a journey
incomplete

Dry stream beds await
a wetness so needed
Then rains from
forgotten memories
come slowly to fill
that which should
be running with
promises to
quench the spirit's thirst

Loneliness bids welcome
There is an abiding
presence that knows
the steps of pilgrims
who need to know

that there is a
caring beyond and
beneath our words
of solitude

Welcome now the deep
love and peace
of One who knows
and feels the
slow beat of
the lonely heart

Loneliness bids welcome
Even when you
know it not
you are held by
the outstretched arms
of an ever seeking
Creator

PAST PRESENT FUTURE

You drift my way often
seeking both spent joy
and leftover sadness
Foolishly you think your
ponderings can repair
what was broken
It is vanity but your
thought-filled mind
pretends there is
some power in
going where you have been

I am the past
and though
you visit often
your journey leads only
to memories that
must remain as
pictures in the
album of your soul
You cannot make them
live again though
hard you try

I whisper
Let the past be the past
Honor it if you will
but seek not to
live there

You peer over the horizon
that seems not so distant
Your vision thinks it can
go there and carry with it
both anticipation and despair

You think if you try hard enough
you might shape
what is yet to be
Plans you make to be
ready for what comes
are meant to be but
readiness accomplished
But you do more than plan
Your blurred vision perceives
it can go ahead and
somehow create reality

I am the future
and you cannot
abide in my presence
for I am the silhouette
of what might be
but these are only shadows

that you might see and
not flesh and blood
of what is real

Ah, at last you have
come to me
I am the present
and I have been waiting
for your late arrival
When you give yourself
to the past or the future
you forgo the power I offer

I am the only place
Where you can really thrive
for my power offers you
real time and real life
Looking ahead with worry
about what might be
robs you of the now
Thinking about what
has been and what might have been
should be short visits
but do not live there
or the moment you
now possess
is left empty

Let me fill you with
my power and presence
Stay with me and

you will really see
instead of simply
passing by

Right now
as you see my words
are you really with me
or has your mind been
caught in the web
of the past
or the beckoning
of the future?

Abide in me and you
will see that I abide
in you
Breathe in the now
in you
Breathe in the now
of life and
gratitude will be
a gift for the taking

I am the present
and that is
all there really is
Live it . . .

INSIDE OUT

(The Need for a Change of Heart)

Inside out
whispered a
voice so close yet beyond
Change you need and
change you shall have
This is a time of markings
so I will turn your
heart inside out

Strange the direction for
accustomed was I
to a heart turned inward
tending the needs of
my solitary life

Sensing this was a time
of needed change
I surrendered to the
call to turn my heart
in an inviting yet
different direction

Pain was the cause of
my willingness to be
given a new path
Selfish had been
most of my loving
but now the time
was for giving
not taking

Other hearts have I changed
the voice stopping me
from longing for a
return to the comfort
of past days

Deep inside I knew
it was a time for the new
Now I would be
looking outward
so as to transform instead
of seeking
to be content with an
easy way of living

Restless to offer love
to dry souls was
my changed heart
The longing to reach out
was a surprise of joy
welcomed like a stranger
bearing gifts

Teach me yet again your ways
for I have listened with
ears full of
needs that were my own
O One who is so close
and yet beyond
in a moment you offer me
a direction I was
not seeking

So I shall do your bidding
for you have turned
my longing heart
inside out
Different shall be my steps
for now they
lead to places out there
not so much in here

What shall you do with
this new direction?
Only you know so I
shall be surprised
by your grace
Change my heart O God
Make it ever new
Change my heart O God
May I be like you

TODAY IS ALL WE HAVE

Don't look to the past
it is not there
and the future is a
wind you
cannot hold

But today is in your grasp
a gift for the holding
Caress its inviting
possibility of *Now*
Do not waste its offering
It desires your
keen attention

The longing to erase
yesterday's remorse
is a futile waste
of today's voice
A voice of reminder
Stay with me

The future is a vision
that can't be seen
with eyes that
need to see what
is happening
so near to you

Now is revealing itself
to your waiting heart
Its beat can only
be heard if you
listen in the present

Listen . . .
Now you are here
Not behind
Not ahead
Be present
It's all
you have

WHAT MATTERS?

To gain seems the
end and the beginning
But loss often fills
the empty place
where my soul asks
the haunting question
What matters?

All my additions seem
at times wrapped
with a bow whose
purpose is to hold
together the reality
that I still do
not have enough

Then I hear a whisper
not heard before
because of an all
too noisy life
What matters?

Why the persistence of
these words that
seem to stalk my
hurried path?

Could it be that
something or someone
from beyond and
below desires
my attention?
Be still and know . . .
Ah the riddle
What am I to know?
A necessary pause
surrounds my
wandering mind . . .

*Know you are but
a child of love's
desire to reflect
a call to a far
too busy world*

*You are a gift crafted
by unseen hands
fashioned by a
divine artist
No item on a list
are you
You are made for
love so that
you may share
that love*

That is
what matters

TEARS OF THE HEART . . . FLOWERS OF HOPE

"They that sow in tears shall reap in joy." Psalm 126:5

They flowed from a place of pain
leaving streaks on a
wounded heart broken by
life's constant need
to be content and full
but empty was
my soul's cup

The tears were ever before me
halting any future
that would bring healing
and a glimmer of hope
Darkness became a companion
whose presence crowded out
the light of tomorrow
that longed to offer
a sunrise of promise

Then came a breaking open
The pain became a kind
of plow digging up the
soil of the past and
making a time for growth
a time for possibilities
a time for new beginnings

Tired tears became the
water that nourished
the hope-filled buds of
a past now ready to
offer a new vision
of what could be

Flowers of hope appeared
as a surprise that
longed to be embraced
The tears became reminders
of how pain could
become a strange preparation
for the growth needed
to be alive and free

THE SECOND CHANCE

The door closed and
the key turned the lock
Shut was my life so
I turned to walk
the way of the past

Then hearing a strange sound
I turned to see
the lock unlock
and there he stood
doing nothing but
look my way

I waited in astonishment
to see what he would do
but there was only silence
and then my wounded mind
knew the silence
was for me

I walked slowly toward
the now unlocked door
He smiled a smile of
waiting love
Then he spoke but
a few words,

Come to me

It was a second chance

THE JOURNEY

Pause a moment and wonder,
From where did I come?
An act of love may have
made you but
that is not what
created you

You were thought up in
the midst of a
cosmic dream
Your arrival was planned
by a divine schemer
who longed for you
to take the journey

At times you feel lost
but that place
is not your destination
for the next turn
is waiting for you
to find yourself
wanted by
the Designer

Discovery is the journey's
end and beginning
To find who you are
is to encounter
your source from afar
This is no road without
direction for you
are always accompanied
by the One who
dreamed you up

Whisper *thank you* to the
wind at your back
It is the presence of a
love that knows you
for it created you for
that love

Feel it Embrace it
Receive it
and for God's sake
seek to give it
So many who are with you
on the journey need
to know what you
now know

God is the journey and
the journey's end

WOUNDED SOUL

The scars are hidden
deep behind senses
that greet a world
where old hurts
are invisible to the
watching eye

Lonely are the moments
where I remember
the source of my wounds
Like a picture in the
album of my life
the remembrance stares
back at me
recalling the past
where the hurt had
its birth

Now I sit with the
old pain and wait for a voice
to explain the lasting
reality that I
long to forget

I will need the touch
of an unseen hand
that wants to offer
healing for that
which I cannot
undo or escape

Ready am I for a freedom
that can only come from
unlocking the
closed door of memories
that haunt me today

Finally I am ready
to receive what I
have neglected in my
tiring efforts to
live with heart
pains that now
need a cure

Do what only you can do
for you understand
my broken past
and you long to
fill the empty spaces
with a private love
that now becomes
personal

GOD'S FATIGUE

Tired they think I'm not
Constant love have I
eternally shared with them
Their forgetting is
an ever-present reality

With the dust I held in
my hands of creation
I shaped them with a hope
that they would remember
to be my own

Soon they ate a fruit
forbidden yet tempting
Like the children they were
I covered their young
and foolish nakedness
with my longing
for them to be more

The story I wrote for them
they failed to read
Writing their own narrative
they broke my tablets
and my heart

Voices of warning
I sent to them
but they seemed deaf

Weary of their wandering
I offered them my heart
starting in a crude cradle
and ending on a lonely cross
After the dark clouds passed
a day of Resurrection dawned
and I waited

Still they go their own way
Give up I will not
though my tiring mind
sometimes thinks it wise
But my heart I so often
share with them
keeps me trying to
help them remember
though forever foolish
they are mine

THERE IS A PLACE OF DEEP PEACE

Like a breeze whose birth
is from a far-off
place where
still waters
invite weary souls
to simply wait

There is a gift for
the taking
offered only to those
whose deep need
speaks to them of
answers not found
in busy words

*Peace that the world
cannot give*
A promise first given
to tired seekers
whose troubles had
captured their
fear-filled hearts

Now that promise can
be yours

From far off that
breeze comes to
those empty places
that need an
assurance not
given by a world
spinning too fast

Peace that the world
cannot give
The breeze speaks
your name
Receive the gift from
afar that is
now so close
Deep Peace

ADRIFT YET AFLOAT

A tide comes from an
horizon beyond sight
It lifts me as if to
take me to an
unknown destination

What are these waters
that leave me adrift
yet afloat?
Surrounded by a sea
of life's movement
I wonder who I am
who is held
by a tide of grace

The wind above the water
whispers a mysterious
verse that includes
You are here at
my beckoning
No driftwood are you
You are my
message in a bottle

Upon a distant shore
my heart suddenly
is washed onto
waiting sands

What words are penned on
that call from afar?
And I see the
mystical message

You are gift
fashioned by unseen hands
No idle thought
are you
Washed ashore you
may seem
adrift yet afloat
But of my making
are you
and love is
your design

Smile
adrift yet afloat
and all because
I sent the message

WHERE IS MY END?

Flickering like the flame
of a slowly burning candle
are those moments I
wonder about the end
the end of the day
the end of sorrow
the end of unanswered questions
the end of my journey
the end

From across a time long spent
I hear words
strange though they seem
I am the Alpha and Omega
the beginning and the end

You whose end came on a
lonely hill between
two lost souls who
wondered what their
end meant
if anything . . .

You now speak into my questions
and the words of hope
meant for pilgrims of the past
who felt alone with
their pondering about the end
Those words are for me

Fear not your end . . .
Your quiet whisper
surrounds me
*Just as the beginning is mine
so is the end . . .
your end
For now live
as if the end matters little
Today with all its joys
and sadness is all
that you need
Stand before your flickering candle
and know that I
am the light of the world
Your end will be yet
another beginning
because I am
the Alpha and Omega*

WELCOME O WANDERER

(The New Year Speaks)

Waiting like a father reaching
for a child's
first awkward steps
Longing as a mother who looks on
helplessly as her child
resists a warning

I reach to you as another
chance to make a
difference in time
You think yourself small in
the vastness of so
many people who walk
past in a pace
as if to arrive at
what matters

What matters is you . . .
You are no accident or
incidental occasion
on a playing field
in some game
All would be different
if you were not here

I greet you . . . again
You matter
Make a difference
I will notice
And the one who
created me . . . and you
will too

TO BEGIN AGAIN

What is this *time*
that we in vain
seek to measure?
Its passing mocks
our slippery quest
to control its flow

Yet once again *time* smiles
our way with a
gentle invitation
Begin again it whispers
as it offers the
gift found in moments
of silent waiting

Not too late for the new
The rhyme seeks a
melody only we can
compose
Waiting is the blank page
of *time's* constant
song of Creation

Begin again...
A chance not to be
wasted amidst
days that become
too ordinary
It is the *time* of
our lives...
Begin again...

IN THIS MOMENT

The bird rests on a limb
. . . the limb of a branch
. . . the branch of a tree
. . . the tree of life
the life is you
that rests on
Mother Earth

The bird will fly away
but not this moment
of notice
The bird is there for her
not for you . . .
unless you make it
a moment

Your vision makes reality
We are not patrons
in a theater with walls
filled with created images
that flash before us
in artificial colors
from afar

We are
well . . .
bird watchers
We are birthed
to pay attention
aware that moments come
from the wings of time

So here is another one
for you . . .
In this moment . . .
a gift for you . . .
Notice . . .
The bird waits but
for a moment

NO OPEN DOORS

Through my limited view
I saw no open doors
Corners were all
I could see
Around the bends of
my vision of
clouds and dust
there were but ends

Beginnings needed a
space filled with
missing hope
Shut was my imagination
Closed was my heart
because time seemed
trapped by
a future dimmed
by locked out
light

Then a hand from beyond
reached for the
closed door
Slowly light seeped
from around the
crack in my
darkness

There were no words yet
the silence spoke
from the new light
and I could hear from
the other side of
the now open door,

The light shines in
the darkness
and the darkness
cannot overcome it . . .

Open the door
all the way
Let your light
shine

Themes from Scripture

Thy word is a lamp unto my feet and a light unto my path.
PSALM 119:105

ON THE JOURNEY OF faith, we soon discover that it can often be dark out there. A light and a lamp sure come in handy when uncertainty is all around. I sometimes remind people who feel in the dark that it has always been dark. According to our scientific discoveries, the known cosmos is made up of 95% dark energy and dark matter. That means all of creation is full of darkness. A solitary candle does not seem so bright until it is the only light in a dark room.

Another Scripture proclaims, "The light shines in the darkness and darkness did not overcome it (John 15:9). While we must acknowledge that in our universe and in our lives, there is a good deal of darkness, we quickly become aware of the need for some light for our paths. Scripture is one of those lamps for the path.

Unfortunately, the Bible can be the most abused and misused book available to us. In one of my other books, I share that the Bible is not a brick. A brick is composed of a mixture that is blended and then put in a mold. The mold is then baked and out comes a composite form that we call a brick. In our contemporary situation, the Bible is often being thrown around like a brick. It is used as a method of striking the point that "I am right, and you are wrong." Our sacred text deserves better than that.

The Bible is more like a grandmother's quilt. She collects pieces that have been saved from various family heirlooms and she lovingly hand stitches them together in a pattern of her own devising.

Some of the old pieces she might not choose to include in the quilt because of their quality, but they are part of the family story, so she includes them. There are some parts of the Bible we might wish were not there: holy wars where women and children are killed, women being considered property, slavery, instructions to stone disobedient children to death, and—depending on your own view, prejudices, and theological posture—certain verses that do not suit our understanding of what faith really is.

That grandmother's quilt is not sown by machine. It is hand quilted. It is not a perfect tapestry, but it reflects the family story. It is meant to be held close and appreciated for what it is, not revered for what it is not. It is the symbol of a sacred but often complex story. It is given for use by the family. It is to be honored but not worshiped.

So what about the Bible being the "inspired" word of God? Inspired means "God breathed." For the Bible to be inspired, it does not mean that it is infallible or without error. In my opinion, as one who has studied the Bible in depth for over fifty years, the power of inspiration comes from the encounter with the text. It is not a matter of simply observing the text as if it were somehow magically infused with something, as if the writers injected it with a hypodermic of power from God. Such thinking leaves room for the Bible to be a kind of "Paper Pope" to be referred to without questioning the meaning of the words.

Jacob, in his famous wrestling match with God beside the River Jabok, encountered a God who wanted to be personalized, not admired from a distance. Jacob's life was forever changed as he became personally aware of the Divine Presence.

An old story that Jacob had listened to from his youth became "his story." The Scriptures are meant to be *a defining story that alters our personal story*. The words from the Bible become more than words when they are "breathed" into our story. The power of Scripture comes not from knowledge of the words but from encounter with the words.

The image of grandmother's quilt is offered as a symbol to convey my understanding of the inspired Word of God. The poems that follow are based on pieces of that quilt. As that quilt surrounded me with its story, I experienced its warmth and meaning for times when I needed some comfort when it was dark. The Bible can not only be a lamp unto our feet but also a quilt that surrounds our need for understanding and comfort.

The poems reflect the many themes we see in Scripture including the need for grace, the desire not to feel alone, the longing for comfort amidst storms, the questions that arise when someone takes their own life, God's fatigue while dealing with wayward children, and a Shepherd's constant watch over sheep who both stay in the fold and those who leave.

You will not find in these words bricks to use as a foundation for a dwelling to keep the world at bay. Hopefully you will discover the comforting grace of a God who longs to make sure that the faith family remembers the ongoing story of a love that will not give up.

So while it may be dark out there, there is a lamp to guide us and a quilt to surround and hold us. May these words help you feel in a very personal way the stitched together, very old and lasting love, of a sacred Grandmother who is also the God who offers light in the darkness

THE LOST GARDEN

The Garden of Eden/Genesis 3

Inviting it was
though forbidden
by a voice
for its power to
entice and destroy

A fruit just out of reach
seemed so close yet far
Another voice offered a
chance to truly
live and let live

What could be the harm
of just a taste?
And so the deed
was done
a quick moment
in time yet altering
a waiting future

Our temptations seem
all so good for the picking
No voice will keep
us from venturing
to taste what
seems like freedom

But the price is high
though hidden by
pleasure's bidding
So we live east of a
garden that bears the name,
Could have been

Careful you should be
echoes that voice
from long ago
So he waits outside
the closed gate
and offers us yet
another chance
to choose

STILL WAITING

"When my people were children, I loved them,
and out of bondage, I called to them."
Hosea 11:1 (Paraphrase)

My children always you are
In moments of your unknowing
I held your hand
My memory of all this lasts
as yours fades quickly
Still I wait

Chords of love surround you
yet you feel constraint
Often you struggle for
release from what seems
like limits to your constant
seeking for freedom

I stand not in your way
I let you go
knowing all too well
the waiting perils
you will face
thinking that I am
no longer needed

Still I wait
My hand reaches to you
longing for your return to
the one who filled you with
that first breath
of the life you now live
thinking it to be yours alone

Imagine in this moment
a time you have forgotten
when I held your hand
and taught you those
first steps as you
stumbled forward
I held you when you fell
and gave your fearful
soul comfort

Grown up and old
you feel often a separation
from that reaching hand
of constant care
Trust not your feelings
Always I am there
Still waiting

DEEP THE VALLEY

Psalm 23

It appeared as my
steps of hope took
me on a path
not of my knowing

Dark was its entrance
as I turned to
find some other way
But there was no other way
so my fear led
me into the darkness
of a valley not desired

The valley has many names
Loneliness
Sickness
Dreams Shattered
Empty Promises
And at its end
there awaits
all manner of death

Long ago some pilgrim
seeking answers
called the valley
the place of shadows
Light seems
but a stranger
not invited

But there need not be
utter loneliness in
the deep valley
for there is One who
knows its winding
paths of mystery

His presence goes before
us as we stumble
It is his valley
for he claimed it
before we arrived

Dark and deep though it be
He is there
He keeps us not away
from the dark paths
but never are we alone

Reach out for His hand
And though it be scarred
it reaches toward you

The valley though deep is
His valley
He made it His from
a lonely hill
where crosses stood

Yes, deep is the valley
but it is filled with
His abiding presence
So hear the words from
long ago
Old are they but they
are full of life
even in the midst
of all our deaths . . .

Though I walk through the
valley of death
you are with me

THERE YOU ARE

"Where can I go from your Spirit? Where can I flee from your presence?" Psalm 139

In moments of deep thought
my mind wanders to
a place of beyond
Doubts have their way
in the midst of
what feels like a
sunset of absence

You are not there
says the rising darkness
And then comes the
whisper that surrounds
me like the warmth
of a grandmother's quilt
Even the darkness is mine

Then the absence is
full of a meaning deeper
than my words
There you are
waiting to offer a
sunrise of hope

The wings of the morning
hold me as I seem to fall
and your promise
surprises me yet again
My fleeing spirit is
caught by a love
that creates life
deeper than any
doubt

I bow my head and
feel an unseen hand
that blesses me in
a silence of
deep peace

You are mine
No worries of an
all to heavy world
can have you
No matter where your
questions may take you
my child
I am there

FEAR NOT

The Lord is my light and my salvation; whom shall I fear?"
Psalm 27:1

Ancient words ask a question
Whom shall I fear?
But my fears are many
Flee away they will not
and often they haunt me
with an abiding presence

Caverns of doubt seem
ever present in my
walk toward the light
Yet there is one who
has taken my fears
into his wounded hands

Longing for my fears
to not be present
an assurance starts
to surround me
and though the fears
remain into the night
there comes one who
holds the light in his keeping
He promises to shine hope
onto my struggling faith

I close my eyes and see
a horizon of promise
that came on a still night
surrounded by
much to fear

Fear not
for I bring you
good news of great joy
Birth pains though they be
I will hold the
promise gently
in my weary hands
and step forward
with a courage that comes
not from within

WATERS OF GRACE

"Come all you who are thirsty, come to the waters." Isaiah 51:1

No price to be paid
This water is not
for your thirst that
comes from a dry day
created by the sun's
draining need to
be noticed

This water is for the
arid places created
by your soul's longing
for a respite from
drinking in the constant
testing that life seems
to demand so often

Come to the waters
whispers the one who
knew you when your mother
held you within
surrounded
by waters of a life
soon to be
given and lived

The one who formed you
knows your thirst
The dry times are noticed
though you may feel alone
in your seeking for
a drink that
will finally give
you solace

Sit now
Drink in
the silence of a
love that waits
to give you that which
you cannot earn
Let the waters of grace
fill the places
carved out by
time's demanding need
to arrive at some unknown destination

Drink now the waters
of healing
given to you for the
dry places that the
one who knows you so well
notices always
Let the waters of grace
quench your thirst
They are for you

WAITING ON GOD

"Those who wait for the Lord shall renew their strength."
Isaiah 40:31

Wanting my seeking spirit
to find rest
I long to feel
assurance in this
present moment

Then comes but one word
Wait
If it came from the
knowledge learned
in my ever-present
desire for certainty
I would not listen

But this request comes
from the One who
tossed the stars
across the fabric
of the heavens and
then called them each
by name

Pausing in my impatience
I chance to ask
If you know all
their names
what is it that
you know mine?

And then my longing heart
feels the answer
in the silence of
my need to know
You are a God
worth waiting for

Those who wait for the Lord
shall renew their strength
O One who crafted me
in a moment of
mystery
I now open my hands
and my soul
and
wait

A YOUNG JESUS PONDERS HIS TWO FATHERS

By myself I look across the
years past
remembering a father who
held me from stable days
to those times
where wood was crafted
by his tired but loving hands

Life ended for him
too soon for my desires
Helpless was I to stop
the veil that covered
him with death's
request that he leave me

Not yet ripe were the fruits
that I will someday
offer hungry souls
who long for a nourishment
not provided by
their hands of labor

Now I sit in the presence of
my other father
who seemed to watch
from a distance

as days passed
and the love I had
for the father
who cared for me
in my growing years
became a memory

Now O father
you whisper to me
Call me Abba
Your parenting draws close
for my time is now at hand
and I fondly remember
the father who held
my hand as I learned to
take those first
steps of childhood

So now I need to hold
your hand
as I walk a road
that leads to a place
where your love for this
weary world
will be made known

Hold me tenderly yet
with a strength
that only you can provide
for I must do
your bidding

Abba father
I remember both
of you and need
what each of you brings
Soon I will offer a plea
for all those who dare
to follow me
Our father who art in heaven . . .
Both of you

A LARGE MAN WITH SMALL THOUGHTS

Mustard Seeds and Leaven/Matthew 13:31–33

Kingdoms needed to topple
Change long awaited
required the loud sound
of crumbling walls
The Past awaited something
very large
And then came words that
seemed to not fill
the empty places
carved away by hope
lost in prayers
not answered
It is like a mustard seed

Silence greeted such
small expectation
Where were the forces
that would crush
the layered evil that
covered dusty dreams?
Speak lofty words of
power and might
was the plea
from hearts long broken
from waiting

*It is like leaven in
the hands of a
woman crafting
a loaf*

What kind of misguided wisdom
could alter a world
so needing something
big and bold?
The future still seemed
held captive by
a past full of fear

Then a large man with
small thoughts
spoke into the
waiting silence
*Give me your little faith
and together we
can change this
vast hurting world
forever*

Trust now the still
small voice
and a kingdom not of
this world
will invade the
present
and make a very
large difference

NO WAY

"Here is a boy with five small barley loaves and two small fish,
but how far will they go among so many?"
The Feeding of the Five Thousand/Matthew 14:13–21

Too hard is the race
before me
Limited is my already
tired spirit
But I lean toward the
distant future
pushing aside the
thought of
No Way

Faith
seems but a
word beyond reach
I cannot drink the water
waiting in a well
too deep for my
dry rope of a life
But I let down my
empty bucket
despite the warning
No Way

Then comes an old story
The crowd hungry for
much more than food
yet time it is for
something to eat
And then comes a whisper
from a full-of-doubt
fear-filled follower
No Way

A smile of assurance comes
from one whose mission
is beyond mere understanding
Give me what you have
he says into the
face of doubt
But words seem empty
and again the answer
No Way

Then the now-called miracle
happens because of
the failure to heed
those haunting words,
No Way
and five loaves and
two small fish
become a meal
for you and me

Feast on the story O
pilgrim on the road
It is for all those times
when we feel
that there is
No Way

The one who lived faith
as he spoke it
looks into our
worried questions
and when we echo
No Way
he says
*Give me the little
you have*

It is food from the past
for our lean and frail faith
In those times when the
clouds of doubt
cast a shadow onto
our struggling spirits
and then
the sun breaks through
and sheds light on
those words,
No Way

And across the years he says
to those who will listen
Give me what you have . . .
It will be enough

WHERE CAN I FIND YOU?

(Searching for Jesus)

Arid is my breath
as this wilderness
greets me in my
search for you
Wet from baptismal waters
you discover your calling
by getting lost
in a desert of
temptation

Thirsty is my parched
soul that seeks water
but there you are
with a lonely woman
whose guilt is heavy
She desires that her
parched life be
bathed with a
water not found
in a well

Shepherd that you are
I journey to the
sheepfold only to
discover your absent watch
Evening's coming darkness
reveals your tired
figure limping back
with a lost lamb
draped over
your shoulders

Finally in your endless journey
you pause long enough
to turn and look
into my waiting eyes
No words are needed
You know that I
too am in need of
your searching love

Here I am
tempted
thirsty
lost
I find you at last
as you find
me

LONELY WAIT

The Prodigal's Father/Luke 15:11–32

Sunsets were his companion
Each end of day
he waited
in front of a house
now vacant
his wayward son
somewhere out there

The road down which
he looked with
an empty stare
seemed to have no end
for it led to
some far country
where a son who
was lost
now dwelled

The longing in his heart
grew with each
dying day

His mind journeying
to that far off place
as he wondered
if his son shared
any of his loss

He turned to go in as
the sun set yet again
But something turned
his tired head
A figure in the distance
seemed to come his way
He knew it was some
dazy daydream
for empty had been
those days of waiting

Then the silhouette came
closer as if to
be looking for something
The leftover sunset illuminated
a broken spirit
as he limped toward
the place he left
so long ago

A hopeful father ran toward
what might be
and embraced the
dream he dreamed
every sunset

The place of loss filled
with waiting love
Apologies rang empty
replaced by a
love that was beyond
rules and regret

He could only whisper
words through his tears
And from an embrace
so long hoped for
he managed to say
*My son who was lost
is now found*

FOREVER THIRSTY

Jesus and the Woman at the Well/John 4:5–30

Parched is the path I take
seeking not just water
but something for the
dryness in my
weary soul

My past hangs heavy not
just around my
drooping shoulders
but it hinders any
hope for a drink
that would at least
cease my seeking thirst

Now another man
again standing in my way
to some peace that
only comes from being alone
His shadow is deep
in the heat of the
morning sun that shines
for others but not for me

His words about water not
from a well but
from one who
looks beyond my past
and into a present
suddenly filled with hope

I leave my bucket beside
a well from whose water
is not for me this day
Within me is a wellspring
of beginnings that
were buried beneath
my dry burden

And now for you
O one who stands
before these words from
a past not yours
but that offer something
for your hidden thirst
Step into the cool shade
of his ever-reaching love
Though from a long-lived
story of a lost woman
searching for something to
quench her deep thirst
this story can be yours

In this moment the water
is for you
Sit by the well
of your longing
and drink

FOOLISH LOVE

(Jesus and the Lost Sheep/Matthew 18:12–14; Luke 15:3–7)

    Foolish was his venture
      leaving the many
        for the one
   Nameless they were not
      Each sheep was
    his own by choice

  He called them and they
     knew the sound
   A voice whose nights
  were spent in vigilance
  All were special though
    there were many

    It was only one
       the stray
  but the one mattered
His love knew no counting
   Into the night he
  went forth with a
  hope born out of
   a restless watch

So now we hear an old
story about a lost sheep
and imagine its meaning
The words are for you
They are given for all
your lost moments
when you think you
know better than
the shepherd

AND NOW

(Reflections of the woman caught in adultery,
as she kneels before Jesus/John 8:1–11)

Only his feet do I see
The dust hides my shame
only to be revealed
by those who would
end my sin and my life

I dare not look up
for I would see
yet another judge who
would expose what I
know so well

There is nothing left
of me but the stain
I am forever condemned
to live or die as
one who has no hope

Hope faded in years past
as I gave myself away
to lonely men
who claimed they needed
an embrace only
I could share

This stranger touches my
bowed head and
lifts my tear-stained face
to see my guilt and my shame
But he says nothing of
judgment only a
look of strange acceptance

An audience of questions
waits in silence to
witness what will surely
be the end of my painful
journey seeking love

Who condemns you now?
Words from the face
of one who looks
into my dry parched soul
Rise to a new life
Go and feel forgiveness
and leave your sin
with me

WHERE ARE THE NINE?

(A poem for Thanksgiving based on the story
of the thankful leper/Luke 17:11–19)

In such a hurry we spend
our lives as if shopping
for some meaning that
so often escapes us
Thankfulness is lost
amidst the clamoring crowd
that fills our personal mall
that we call *today*

Bring to mind the old story
of one who remembered
his forgetting
On the way to someplace else
he stopped and turned
and his turning made
all the difference

Kneeling
this thankful pilgrim
looked up to see
the source of his life
now made whole
only to be greeted by
haunting words

Where are those who forgot
to say *thank you*?

Now the long-ago story
becomes yours
No matter where you
planned to travel
on your hectic journey
that so often leads
to a tiring end . . .
stop and turn

Let your heart if not
your seeking body
kneel at the feet
of One who longs
to give you healing
for your too busy
neglected soul

It is thanksgiving time
It is a moment of pause
to remember the One
who gives us the
very breath of life
Now is the time
to turn and look up
and whisper,
Thank you!

FREE AS I LONG TO BE

(The Lost Sheep/Luke 15:3–7/John 10:27–28)

Free as I long to be
The memory of my wandering
still blurs my vision of
a desire to have
the more that is
not mine to have

You look at me knowing
the path is mine
to choose
No escape is blocked
by your persistent
watch of my
wayward heart

The assurance of peace
should cease the
constant lure of
what might be
on the waiting trails
of what seems to
be happiness

Still you look my way
noticing always
my leftover longing for
that freedom that still
calls to me

You will let me go again
will you not?
The stale lessons
from my wilderness
journey remains buried
in my seeking spirit

O Shepherd of the sheep
keep me in
your watch
I am lost without your
tending even when
I pretend to be free

Call my name again for
you know it well
I am yours even
when I am not
I remain a sheep of
your own fold . . .
free as I long
to be

CALM MY STORM

(Jesus calms the sea. "Peace, be still." Mark 4:39)

A story frozen in time
as is my unsteady
boat of a life
Long ago you spoke
into fear-filled
faces a word of
calm

No clouds on a distant
horizon cause
the storm I face
The wind and waves
are within my
soul's disturbed
waters

Can I call on you
to calm the gale
of my troubled
spirit?

Is your reach also
for the rough waters
of my shallow faith
that needs your words
Peace, be still

Speak them to me
O master of wind and wave
Then I will wait upon
your words of comfort
so that the sea of
my all too stormy
spirit may receive
the calm you
long to bring . . .

Peace, be still

GRACE TOO LATE?

"But the pot he was shaping from the clay was marred in his hands; so the potter formed it into another pot, shaping it as seemed best to him." Jeremiah 18:4

Misshapen was my longing
to spin so fast
to get somewhere
Then my all too hurried
spirit slowed to
a troubling pace

Backward I could not go
and future turns seemed
without certain direction
Lifeless though my words
something stirred within
but came from beyond

It was a kind of touching
from another's notice
My quieted awareness
sensed I had
ceased the turning
of my now
settled self

Unseen hands gripped my
thought that all
was finished in my
lost sense of knowing much
And then the spinning
resumed but
with different intent

The strange renewal
had a sound
and feel to it
My questioning spirit had
a mystifying sense of
some power that
had a shape
to it

What kind of potter is it
who takes what
for a while seemed
not his
but made it so
and then turns it
with wet muddy love?

What form will I become
held by these
daring hands
that never give up
even when I do?

Stop now and listen
to your own
spinning
Let it be a movement
toward a grace
that remains
and always will be
amazing

BLURRED VISION

"For now we see in a mirror dimly, but then we will see face to face. Now I know in part; then I will know fully, even as I have been fully known." I Corinthians 13:12

Blurred is our vision
as we long to see
the truth of our lives
The image in the mirror
seems distant and
who we are remains
a mystery in time

But there is a promise
that comes from long ago
Though blurry is our vision
in the mirror of the present
a light will shine
in the darkness
and we shall see
a sight of surprise

We will be *known* as if
for the first time
Face to face is the
promise from one
who was the
human face of God

So peer now into
a mirror dim
for life withholds
many of the answers
to the questions
we long to know

A day will arrive when
the one who smiled through
the pain and joy of life
will look our way
and bid us come to
him though we are
burdened and heavy laden
for he longs to give us rest

Walking beside us though
we see him not
with our limited vision
is the one whose face
we shall see and
all blurred vision
will be cleared

SO LOST BUT FOUND

(Losing someone to suicide/Matthew 18:2–14/Luke 15:3–7)

We lose so much
and fear that the loss
is final
But there is one who
does not take the loss
as the last answer

He is the Shepherd who
knows each sheep
by name
Leaving the many
he seeks the one
who wonders away
from the light

When our loss seems
something that will
always remain
the Shepherd keeps
on seeking
until he finds
the one lost lamb

Not knowing the hidden
reasons that the
lost one strayed
we too are lost
The Shepherd cares
more for the lost
than he does
for the reasons

Finding in the darkness
the lost sheep
the Shepherd gently
lifts him onto
his shoulders
and takes him to
a home that
seems far away

But the place of rest
for the wounded
and the lost
is very near to
the heart of
the ever-seeking Shepherd

The lost sheep may be
lost to us
who seem left behind
but not to the Shepherd

who finds the
sheep and holds
him in the midst
of unanswered questions

The Good Shepherd never
gives up hope
He knows the lost
sheep's name
and now claims him
as his own

Advent and Christmas

> "Now, here, you see, it takes all the running you can do, to keep in the same place. If you want to get somewhere else, you must run at least twice as fast as that!"
>
> THE RED QUEEN IN LEWIS CARROLL'S
> *THROUGH THE LOOKING GLASS*

DOES THE ABOVE SOUND familiar as you ponder what happens in our busy culture just after Halloween? The orange facades created by pumpkins and left-over witches faces are quickly replaced by the red and green of artificial Christmas trees. In stores, the sound of Jingle Bells plays in the background as boxes are being unloaded that contain various size images of the jolly old elf ready to whisk you into the "most wonderful time of the year."

It is indeed an irrational season filled with too many presents to purchase with sometimes too few dollars. We are told by those who study us that it is the not just the "most wonderful time of the year," but also the most stress-filled time for many who long to make it "the best Christmas ever."

In these poems for Advent and Christmas, I want to reclaim the busy holiday time filled with the often too loud sounds of the season and offer in its place what Madeline L'Engle calls the *real* irrational season:

> This is the irrational season
> when love blooms bright and wild.

> Had Mary been filled with reason
> there'd have been no room for the child.
> (A Cry Like a Bell)

Thank God, Mary was not filled with answers to her questions but with a faith that took a big chance. Unfortunately, that is not our problem with our all-too-filled lives as we step toward a waiting manger. We are filled with the *too much* of the season; too much desire, too much need to reclaim a Christmas of the past, too much envy of those who have more, and too much of too much.

Allow these poems to remind you of the irrational way God intervenes in our lives. We have overlaid the all-too-simple story of two homeless people in a barn with our need to have Christmas instead of letting Christmas have us.

For our busy holiday culture, time is counted by the number of shopping days until Christmas. For the Christian pilgrim there is a stop sign before we get to the *This Way to Christmas* flashing light. It is not even a yield sign telling the traveler to slow down; it is a sign that says, "Stop right now and pause to remember what is coming!" The answer to that call to remembrance is not found up on the rooftop but rather down deep in the heart of God.

This pre-season is Advent. The word literally means "coming." The light that is coming is not the light of a freight train called the Christmas rush but a dim lantern that burns in a stable. The season of Advent is a season of caution to remind us that if we are not careful, we will miss the light that will shine over a manger. The lantern's gentle light can be overshadowed by the glare of very bright Christmas lights.

In the old days, Advent was considered a little Lent and was a time of examination and repentance. Those old days are up and gone due to our need not to spend too much time on the heavy burden that is confession.

A kind of compromise is what is left of Advent. It is a time to at least get ready and prepare rather than just having a surprise party on Christmas Eve. If the party is to happen, the God of the ages wants us to prepare a way in the wilderness of our busy season. Notice I say *our* busy season for it seems we have taken over Christmas and returned it to its ancient origins.

Rumor has it that we have no idea when Jesus was born, so some Pope a long time ago grew tired of all the celebrations that paid homage to the Sun, the Winter Solstice, and Dionysus, the Greek god of wine, whose birthday was marked on December 25 and whose festival was marked by wildness and excess. He therefore decided that Jesus' birthday should be December 25, and we would have our own party celebrating the birth not of the "Sun" but the "Son."

The vote is still out if we have possibly not overturned his edict and gone back to some of the pre-Christian stuff. Advent is the stop sign so that we can pause and reflect and get ready for the original child of Christmas, no matter when he was born.

I hope you will make use of these Advent poems as a time to ponder and slow down. There are also poems that shed some imaginative light on the "best Christmas ever." That Christmas happened when the world was too full to listen, too tired to stay up late, and too weary of waiting for God to finally come through on promises made over the centuries.

Shepherds and star searchers discovered that God's timeline was not the world's measure. So, though it was a surprise, that silent night ended up being the best Christmas ever. May these words help you experience a very wonderful irrational season.

IT CAN'T BE

Barren was a world
whose emptiness
seemed to be forever
It can't be
was the
echo from a darkness
that covered everything

Promises broken and
exiles too frequent
became the narrative
of a story with
no hope filled ending
It can't be
Again came
the voice of despair
reminding people
who no longer expected
much of anything
Then came strange words
cried into a wilderness
of constant waiting,
Prepare the way
But weary voices could
only whisper,
It can't be

But then Mary said
Yes
and a bewildered Joseph
muttered words of
strange acceptance
and sleepy shepherds heard
an invitation from
the stars
and a reluctant innkeeper
led strangers to
a barn out back
and seekers from a
distant land
found not what they
were looking for

At last a tired-of-waiting God
spoke into the
long lasting words
that seemed to be
what would always be
It can't be

But a sort of divine
laughter offered
a surprised world
new words,
It can be!
A little child
shall lead them

DESTINED TO FLY

Legs in the air looking
toward a waiting sky
I dreamed of flying
The swing was but
a moment in time . . .
a place to make plans
for a coming adventure

Growing up the fantasy
lost its power
The worries of tomorrow
filled my mind
with constant motion
and gone was
the hope of letting go
and soaring toward
the clouds

Then came a reminder
of a child who
offers me a chance
to journey toward
still waiting arms
that reach down
from Heaven's longing
to hold me

Come fly with me
whispers this child
whose beginnings were
so grounded that
a tired world
no longer believed
in letting go and soaring

O child of Bethlehem
descend to us we pray
for we are too heavy
to remember days
of wishing to reach
toward the heavens
for a moment of release

Emmanuel—God with us
So in this season of
the child
sit again in the
swing of possibility
and let Christmas
take you toward
a heaven of love
and surprise

WHICH WILDERNESS?

"A voice cries in the wilderness, 'Prepare the way of the Lord.'"
Isaiah 40:3

Why does the cry need to
come in the wilderness?
Better the voice sound
from a mountain top
Its echo then would
resound for all
to hear

But some divine wisdom
chooses to make it
not so known
Seeking must be the
way to find the way
A strange figure will
again invite the seeker
to pay attention

Busy are would-be pilgrims
so a necessary wilderness
will contain seeds of a birth
that can only be
found in the place
where busyness is
not welcome

Where is your wilderness?
Dreams unfulfilled...
Promises forgotten...
Hopes abandoned...
Faith too distant?
To which wilderness
does the cry need
to come this season?

Why the wilderness? some ask
The reason resides in
the need for us pilgrims
to know that love can
live in barren places

God is near in the wilderness
for those who will
give attention to the
journey whose end
leads to a manger

Which wilderness needs a
voice to announce
that though the way
seems absent of love
a flower of hope
will bloom
in the wilderness?

Prepare the way of the Lord...
for the world...
for you...

PREGNANT PAUSE

Waiting for Joseph to
complete wedding plans
she found herself filled
with unexpected
joy and fear

Alone with nothing but
a pregnant pause
Mary leaned into a
promise beyond
any words of wonder

Her waiting begun on
this night of an
angel's voice
left her hoping
that understanding would
overcome fear

Her pause was only
overcome by a
deep feeling that soon
a world longing for
a rebirth of hope
would share in her surprise

Her hands reached down
to a soon-to-grow
body now filled with
a long-awaited promise
It was a
pregnant pause
that would change
everything

INTO THE LONGING

Crying out in a wilderness
of questions unanswered
is a longing to know
that the path which
goes through the darkness
leads to the light

Buried like some treasure
in our fields of
a life that becomes
too ordinary
we long to discover
a hidden wholeness
that holds us

And then comes another voice
not of our own
Prepare the way in
the wilderness
A crying out of a
coming one
who longs to care for
all who will receive
his offer

The treasure no longer hidden
waits for our finding
Emmanuel is no title
preserved in ancient words
It is made real
in the midst of
all our wilderness journeys
God is with us

But listen O pilgrim
and hear what
now comes into your
longing
God is with . . . you

IN NEED OF FILLING

Empty was his life
but full was his inn
So into their tired eyes
he looked with
both pity and remorse
They were
in need of filling
those two who
seemed lost in
the night
So he found room

Still lost in wonder but
full of lingering questions
he did all he could
with limping faith
Trusting the dream
he stumbled into
a stable that seemed
to provide a strange welcome
Joseph was
in need of filling

Fear still held her in
its grip along with
the strange faith
brought to her
by a voice breaking
open her heart
She was to receive a
child of mystery
And now, looking into
the eyes of waiting animals
Mary was
in need of filling

And now you who hear
this story from
a night long ago
must ask into what
vacancies of your life
are you
in need of filling

For if you are too full
the story is a
fairy tale of sorts
but
if you are
in need of filling
then a loving Father
will fill you
with the love
of his child

SEEKING JOY

"In the beginning was the Word ... and the Word became flesh
and dwelt among us" John 1:1–5

A Word from long ago
searching for a void
to be filled
Creation happened from
a thought that became
all that was to be

Stars whose names were
known before they
were named by mortals
witnessed the measure
of time as
it unfolded

Though full of moments
of Creation
there still remained
an empty place
caused by a dream
not yet fulfilled

So a solitary star whose
name was yet to be
appeared on an horizon
brought close by
a need to know
that the Creator
cared

So for all those seeking joy
know that the star
still shines
as it did on a night
of silence long ago
The star's light was
a message of promise

It was the Word spoken
at the dawn of
Creation
and the Creator became
father of a son
His message was to fill
the silence for
all those seeking joy

The Word became flesh
and dwelt among us

Seek joy
His star shines
for you

HIS EYES SEE ME

(Mary looks into the face of her child)

His eyes see me . . .
Waiting have I been
since the voice
of the evening told
me of your coming

Fear filled me before
your presence did
Who am I to carry
this mystery?
Such a weight should
be borne by one
stronger that I

Yet now your eyes see me
and into my heart
your vision calls
a waiting name
Mother
O son of the stars
that shine this night
you are mine
but you are not

You are the world's child
I only hold you for
a precious moment
But now your eyes see me . . .
only me
I will share you too soon
but now I hold you
as you hold me

Now you who read this
Close your eyes . . .
He has come for
you
He sees *you* . . .
Emmanuel

LIMPING TOWARD A MANGER

(A poem of hope for those struggling at Christmas)

Limping toward a manger
whose presence seems
far away
Doubts and trials may weigh
you down along with
the burden of
unanswered questions

Then a whisper reaches down
to your weary soul
Be reminded of
mysterious grace
It came in a
surprising moment
in time when
the world was too dark
and the night was too silent

Then two weary pilgrims
also needed
mysterious grace
Joseph was filled with
leftover doubt about
being an adopted father

Mary was full of life
but empty of
answers as to why
they too limped
toward a manger

What kind of deliverance
could come from
No room
for needed love
How could the lonely
of heart
be healed by
what seemed to be
the absence of
those who even cared?

But to you who now
limp toward a manger
know that he again
waits for you
His arms reach up
from his crude cradle
of mysterious grace
and his eyes of divine
love look into
your pain and
your doubt

He is the child whose
birth comes into
the silent night of
questions unanswered
and his star still
shines into
your darkness

You are not alone
Though sometimes
you feel so
He comes again for you—
and your limp
He is the child
of mysterious grace

NO SURPRISE

A surprised maiden waiting
for a promised wedding
could barely take in
what was soon to
take her in
Mary would give birth to
God's promise

Full of doubt a now
lost Joseph could
only wrestle with his
angel dream
But upon awakening
he was surprised
to feel his questions
answered

But God was not surprised
for long had been
the burning desire
to become one of
his own
The arrival would be meager
but for sure
no surprise

IS IT TOO FULL?

Nazareth was too full
of rumors and suspicion
to risk even a moment
of belief in the
impossible

For what seemed like a
never-ending night
Joseph was too full
of sadness and hurt
to take even a chance
on a mystery message

Herod was too full of
envy and power
to even think of
another king who
would be nothing but
a threat

An inn was too full
to take in God's
strange way of saving
a world that
was too full
of the death of hope

And now are you too full
of shopping days
or leftover grief
of worries of what might be
or lingering doubts
or promises broken?
Pause now and know
that it has always
been *too full*
But God reaches down
to you and
seeks to prepare room
for birth to happen
in your too full life

IT'S ABOUT TIME

It's about time
to ponder if divine
thought could really
be wrapped tightly
in a feeding trough

It's about time to
reason with the
Creator of all time
about why in God's name
would a long-awaited hope
come in the form
of flesh in a barn

It's about time
to remember a
bewildered couple
who took a chance on
dreams and promises
and ended up rescuing
you and me

It's about time
to kneel like surprised shepherds
to follow a star that
leads to light for our darkness
to allow Christmas to
hold you like Mary
held him

It's about time
to allow God's love
for you to be
born into the
manger of your heart

Isn't it about time
for you to realize
how far love will go
and to discover that
on a silent night
God whispered to
you and the world
It's about time?

MARY PONDERED

"Mary treasured these things and pondered them in her heart."
Luke 2:19

O child of promise
I hold you close for
one day I must
let you go

A voice in the night
promised impossible things
and now I nurse a
long-awaited hope
What shall become of you?

Joseph's sleepy eyes
found answers to
a lingering question
and he held me close
knowing we would
be surrounded by
eyes of doubt

A manger waits your
fragile warmth
and a world awaits
your gentle strength

How I sense more
than this moment
only your father knows

Your eyes close in sleep
while expectant time
waits for you
to change the story
of what has been

All I can do is ponder
and surround you
with cradling love
Your journey is already
beyond my imagining

Your future is in the
hands of a distant
father who uses a
simple accepting girl
who in a moment
said *Yes*
*Let it be according
to you will*
Words that came
from deep in my
wondering heart

So be it . . .
O God who must
always be beyond

my understanding
he is your child
So in my pondering
I know that you
love him even more
than I do

SLEEP BETHLEHEM

Sleep Bethlehem your streets
are now empty
but full is the night
Evening found them lonely
and looking for shelter
from questions that filled
their wondering hearts

Finding only a world's *No*
they now rest in the
abode of animals who
must notice how strange
the cry of a child
is in their cold
but welcoming home

Little notice there is of
this night
by those who rest
in your meager town
but when the sun arises
to announce a new day
all will know of your name

You are least among the land
of prophets and promises
but now you are more
than all the forgotten
hopes of your people
who find answers only
in their dreams

Sleep Bethlehem for this night
the heavens are awake
The humble abode you
unwittingly offer will
arouse a future alive
with promises fulfilled

Sleep now comes to them,
tired from a journey
whose end they could
not imagine but
their faithfulness
has changed everything

Rest O city of David
your namesake is
awakened by the surprise
of all time
So sleep this night
for you will never
rest the same again

Even the stars cannot
claim their usual night slumber
They shine into your
sleepy streets
for they know what
you shall soon learn . . .

Emmanuel . . . God is with
your little town
so rest well . . .
The whole world will
awaken with you
and dawn will break
on a New Creation

WHAT IF?

What if Creation's waters
had not gone so far
and then stopped at
a divine voice that said,
Enough?

What if voices of warning
had not been shouted
by weary prophets who
longed to open
the closed ears of
an unfaithful people?

What if the holy past
had not grown tired
of waiting for a
sign that would
alter the sadness
and hope of a
needy world?

What if Mary had said *No*
or if Joseph had not
listened to a night
voice of permission

or if sleepy shepherds had
imagined that voices
from the stars were
but night dreams
or if stargazers had
taken a wrong turn?

What if you who read
these words now
hear only an old story
about a strange birth
and deem it a kind of
sweet tale of
times gone by?

What if this year the
old story takes
root in your soul
and blossoms into
a Christmas rose
whose beauty and fragrance
changes everything?

What if? can be . . .
Believe it
Trust it
Live it

LISTEN TO THE QUIET

Mary listened to the quiet
after a thunderous
announcement telling her
that she would carry
the weight of the world
which would lighten
the burdens of
broken hearts

Joseph listened to the quiet
after words that
seemed loud
asking him to be
an adopted father
who would shield
Mary from whispers
of scandal

Shepherds listened to the quiet
as always on a night
that seemed long in
their keeping of sheep
until voices broke
their waiting silence
telling their weary
lives that now

a child would bring
hope to a
fear-filled world

Stargazers listened to the quiet
after long years of
seeking answers to
questions they asked
of the heavens
And then came a
daring word of direction
Go

And now you must listen
to the quiet
to fill the longing
of your heart
The quiet is full of
a story that needs
to be told to all
who will listen
to the quiet

WHO NEEDS CHRISTMAS?

Who needs Christmas?
The broken hearted
looking for a
faint light
do

Those who lost a love
when death's call
came too soon
do

All who are too full
of shopping days
but who feel empty
do

Smiling faces wanting
someone to thank
for so much
do

Busy people who get
lost in the rush
of the season
do

Who needs Christmas?
All who want to believe
that a great big God
became small on
a silent night
long ago
do

Who needs Christmas?
Wait in this moment
Listen to the question
Ponder the gift because
Christmas needs you

Lent and Easter

"Lent is the most important time of the year to nurture our inner life. It is the time during which we not only prepare ourselves to celebrate the mystery of the death and resurrection of Jesus, but also the death and resurrection that constantly takes place within us. Life is a continuing process of the death of the old and familiar and being reborn again into a new hope, a new trust and a new love. The death and resurrection of Jesus therefore is not just an historical event that took place a long time ago but rather an inner event that takes place in our own heart when we are willing to be attentive to it."

Henry Nouwen, *Bread for the Journey*

"I always get to where I am going by walking away from where I've been."
... "Rivers know this: there is no hurry. We shall get there someday."

A.A. Milne, *Winnie the Pooh*

So a stuffed bear with a heart lets us know that Lent is a time to ponder walking away from where we have been to get to someplace else. The old word for that is *repentance*, which literally means *to turn around*.

And yes, rivers have a mind of their own and remind us that Lent is meant to be a slow journey that will get us to Easter, but we must pay attention and, if need be, stand in the waters of the river of grace.

For me Lent is the necessary wilderness, and who wants to walk through a wilderness? But as I have shared with so many in my role as pastor for fifty-two years, life's detours take us through the wilderness.

When I hear people ask the "Why" question, I listen carefully first, for no one wants or needs a quick platitude when surrounded by the loneliness that comes from being in the desert of life's unfairness. Then, if appropriate, I remind them of how much wilderness and exile there is in the Bible.

The authentic spiritual journey runs through the wilderness. The wilderness is a place of questions, but it is also a place of learning.

Lent is a season to pay attention and ponder our limitations. Traditionally it is a call for self-examination and repentance, not popular themes these days. So, if it seems like a necessary wilderness, so be it. According to the Christian way of things, we need it.

To put it in simple terms, life is wonderful and a gift, but we get dirty living it, and there is a need for a bath. We baptize babies to remind us that we are accepted and loved by grace. But even then, we are called to remember that later we will need those same waters to help us get clean, the cleansing water of repentance.

Recalling the theme of this book, "For God's sake pay attention," I am reminded of what the Reverend Gordon Cosby called "the Golgotha Bypass." It is the temptation to hurry by Lent to get to the Easter party.

It is one reason that years ago someone changed Palm Sunday to Palm/Passion Sunday. It seems that people showed up for the parade where children would joyfully sing "Hosannas," but after the "waving of palm branches Sunday," they would often skip the washing dirty feet scene, the "one of you guys is going to betray me" episode, the "I don't know that guy rooster in the background" drama, and the "Abba, where the hell are you when I need you," cry—the Golgotha Bypass.

So just in case that bypass is taken, we now cram some of the "passion" into the end of the parade and do a two for one: Palm/Passion Sunday. Skip the wilderness and let's get to the sunrise of

Easter. God, who planned all this, must think we need some preparation time in the necessary wilderness to fully appreciate the joy of Easter. So, instead of the road sign that reads, "This way to the Golgotha Bypass," there is the flashing sign that asks us to take the road less traveled.

It is the road called Lent. The journey is a time for pondering our human limitations and a pause before the coming promise of Easter Resurrection. Switching metaphors, Lent is a time for a spiritual diet so that we can hopefully lose some of the emotional weight we have gained from living like we are the "the master of our fate and the captain of our soul." Life's challenges will provide wilderness, but this time we are purposefully invited into the wilderness in order to spend some quality time with Jesus.

We remember Jesus started his own journey in the wilderness, where he encountered the same temptations we wrestle with: the easy way, the ego way, and the "I am God and you are not" way. We need some doing without—whether it be forgoing chocolate cake or giving up judging everyone for not being like us. No wonder they are called Lenten "disciplines." Giving up is not easy these days. Ah, so that's why it's called wilderness. So be it.

My wife, who is an avid flower gardener, taught me that vines need a trellis to grow as desired. In the world of spiritual disciplines, the offer is to establish a Rule of Life. The word *rule* comes from the same word that is the root of *trellis*. In other words, Lent is a time to drag out the trellis if we become aware that we have done some growing wild. The old call for "living a Holy Lent" is because our human condition requires a trellis. That is why we hear the invitation to read Scripture, fast, attend holy orders, and yes, repent.

So, what follows are some poems about the Lenten journey along with some poems celebrating the Easter promise. As suggested earlier, Lent is a good time to use these poems as a way to pause and reflect, and if necessary, to walk away from where we have been. Hopefully we can pay attention to the learning that comes from the wilderness so that we can rejoice even more when it's time to party.

Yes, Winnie the Pooh, rivers know there is no hurry, and when we get there, an empty tomb awaits us, but for the Christian pilgrim, the river runs through a necessary wilderness. The journey calls us to pay attention, for God's sake.

Before you step into the poems for Lent and Easter, let me share a very personal story that helps shed light on the Lent/Easter path. Years ago, I had officiated at three funerals in a row. I was tired but it was time to prepare the Easter sermon. I was not feeling very Easterly. After I finished the committal at the cemetery for the third funeral, I walked to my car and there he was bobbing in the breeze. It was the Easter Bunny smiling at me.

I walked towards the large balloon and noticed it was attached by a silver string to a small gravestone. I read the inscription and realized it was the grave of a small child. Some grieving parents had placed the plastic bunny there to somehow claim a left-over love for a tragic ending. And then my tiredness and yes, bitterness, kicked in.

As I gazed at the rabbit's face, I thought, "What do you have to smile about?" Then, just below the bobbing bunny, I noticed a stone statue of Jesus kneeling in prayer. My sadness deepened, and I looked at Jesus and said, "Why don't you get up and do something about a world where children die and parents have to put fake bunnies over the graves to simply get by?"

With an attitude like that, I was sure lost to any Easter message. Then the same wind that moved the bunny moved me. This is what I heard in the breeze: "I did get up, Jody. I got up for that child at your feet. I got up for all who grieve, especially for parents of children who buy bunnies to ease their pain. You go home and write that Easter sermon, and you tell all who will hear that I 'got up.'"

The Resurrection waters of Easter run through the wilderness, but we do "get there." And, yes, I did go home and write that sermon: "The Stone-Faced Jesus and the Plastic Bunny." Thanks be to God; he did get up.

LIGHT'S JOURNEY

Beginning in the shadows
a yearning brings
a hope born in the
deep recess of love's
need to see the
light of promise

Souls that feel the
desire to turn
and discover a new
direction that
would bring freedom
now sense a
needed birth

Tired are our old ways
that seemed so true
but proved to be
dead ends
on the road
of desires now spent

Light breaks into the
shadows cast by
deceptions that
promised instant happiness
but ended up empty

Waiting is a peace that
only comes from
letting go of our
struggle to gain
fulfillment in
pleasures that proved
to be hollow

Let me hold you . . .
Receive the light
I offer from
the source of all that
is good

Light's journey leads to
my waiting arms
My love can fill
your valleys
of shadows
both big and small

Come to me . . .
I will give you rest

ON HIS KNEES

(The thoughts of Simon Peter as Jesus washes his feet)

> We left nets hanging
> and a father alone
> Not for this did we
> leave so much
>
> On his knees he looks
> up at me
> those eyes
> Not my feet Never
> Rise up from such
> a posture
>
> We thought you a deliverer
> not a slave to
> wash dirt from feet
> What kind of kingdom
> is this where
> towels are given
> rather than chains
> released?

I shall walk away from
such servitude
But your stare captures
me yet again
My words are dry in
my mouth as
as you say that
this is the way

What can change down there
on your knees?
Then you say that from there
you will be lifted up
But such lifting will
only bring you down

You hand me the wet towel
and bid me to kneel
As I do
do likewise
and your soft smile
bathes my soiled
soul

So now on my knees
I will again follow you
What kind of love
must this be?

MY HEART REACHES OUT

(Jesus looks down on Jerusalem)

My heart reaches out
but you walk away
City of a broken past
you are lost in
your grief as
you fail to see
the dawn of
a new chance

The darkness of your
forgetting blinds
you to the light
I offer
Ancient words of
prophets are but
dust under your feet
and you walk the
path of no hope

My arms reach out
to you but you
turn away as if
I am a stranger
who does not know
your hurt-filled story

My salty tears are
reminders of the
deep desire I have
to bring you home
But your tiresome
journey has taken
you far from me
and I fear
you will
fail to grasp what
could be yours

Still I will come
to you
knowing you will
again walk away
My father's persistence
is long in its
constant reach

You will be the
death of me
but still as I
look down upon
your desperate need
I will offer what
is in my heart
It will have to
be enough . . .

and it will be
though now you
know it not . . .

But later all will know
For now
my heart reaches out . . .

WHAT KIND OF LOVE?

What kind of love
looks up and not down?
Dirt on his hands
gathered from one
who would soon deny
his friendship
and his love

What kind of love
seeks humility rather
than praise
and offers the sound
of pouring water
and not the applause
of those who
would offer praise?

What kind of love
looks into the
questioning eyes of
resistant followers
who wonder what
kind of king
would do such
a thing?

What kind of love
would rise from
the stance of a slave
and go to a table
to offer strange words
broken for you?

What kind of love
do you now seek?
Still he asks from
years long past
*Will you follow
such love?*

What kind of love?
God so loved
the world that
he washed feet . . .
That kind of love

FINALLY OR NOT

(The Triumphal Entry)

Finally the answer to
our forgotten hope
comes into the crowded
streets of our lonely
lives that have
waited so long

He looks toward us
from his humble
and all too small fold
as if he knows
the questions that
echo in the midst
of our Hosannas

Is he finally the one
or not?
We hoped for more
anticipating a victory
of royal proportions
Now we wonder at this
meager offering

Yet we hold out our
empty hands and
offer them with a
reach that longs
for this surprise
to be God's unexpected
gift so long awaited

Then the parade of sorts
pauses in its slow
but steady march
He looks toward that
God-forsaken hill
outside the walls
of our tired misery

What hope is there at
that place of death
where our captors have
nailed both future and flesh?
Still we will shout into
his peering eyes
that seem to both
look beyond and into us
for we know not
what else to do

Is he finally the one
or not?
A question so long awaited
now asked

Yet we will trust
O God that
only you know
the answer.

LONELY GRACE

(Looking at Jesus' Cross)

How alone can a
solitary soul be?
Alone is a word
not able to hold
the broken heart's
silent song

Hosannas now are
but a cruel reminder
of how fleeting
promises not fulfilled
can haunt one
who brought a
kingdom not of
this world

The weight of pieced flesh
is slight compared
to the burden of
an effort to save
a people who
fail to see
the cost of love

So now cast your
wandering vision
on this lonely scene
from long ago
He did it for you
who now pause
at a scene that
changed everything

The question left hanging
in the dark clouds of
a day of death
is
*Has that change
changed you?*

That day of lonely grace
is for the healing
of those moments
where there are
no answers and
you think you
are alone

Lonely grace
It is for you

PIETÀ

(Mary holds the body of Jesus after the Crucifixion)

>Playing as a child that
>day you fell against
>the rocks on the
>hillside of Nazareth
>I held you as you wept
>and watched the red
>of life seep from
>your wound

>Now I hold you fallen
>again upon the rough
>landscape of a world
>not yet ready for you
>O my son how empty of life
>you now are because
>you were too full of
>your father's love

>Some angel's voice now
>so distant on this
>tortured hill of death
>told me of your coming

Pounding like nails in my
hearing is only your cry
of dying so alone
for heaven must be empty

Look what they have done your
body so torn from the
hate you came to quiet
and now that quiets you
Some stranger offers you his
own tomb of death
for I have nothing to
give you but my tears

EVERYTHING WAITS

(A poem for Holy Saturday)

Words still linger
in the early morning mist
It is finished
Those he called friends
are hidden away
and waiting
for they know
not what

A heavy stone covers
a waiting darkness
that now holds
one who claimed
to be the light

Tired guards wait for
morning light
so they may return
to yet another duty
to keep a rugged peace
that never seems to happen

And the God he seems
to have lost
in the midst of
words of forsakenness
is waiting . . .
Waiting for what?

Everything waits this day
for tomorrow
all will be changed
The waiting will end
in a moment of
new beginnings

And the God who will be
found worth waiting for
will speak words to
the sunrise and say,
*The waiting is over
Arise my child*

THERE IS A WAY

(A poem of Resurrection)

Endings speak of a
forever that buries
deep into waiting
of our questions
without answers

Darkness so desires
a lasting victory
But there is a way
through what seems
to be a path
with sudden endings

From shadows whose
silhouette portrays
an image of death
there appears a light
which reveals a
way through
all darkness

Resurrection cannot be
contained in a tomb
whose finality
is a cosmic pause . . .

There is a way

The way is through a
valley deep with
a longing for a
meaning not found
in mere words

So God who looks
beyond paths that
seem to end at
waiting graves
speaks a word beyond
our words

Resurrection it was the
word upon his lips that
sunrise of long ago
No death could hold
his love that
offers new beginnings

And now for you and for
a world of need
he speaks into all
the silences of
our little and
big deaths,
Come to me . . .
There is a way

DEATH'S LAMENT

So long I have kept watch
at a door whose
key alone
I possess

But now this upstart
divine avatar
dares rob
me of my
prize

I watched as they stored
his broken body
in one of
my tombs-
And once again
I
slammed the door

And now on this third day
a terrible sunrise
seems to burn away
my shadowy
power

O the sadness I feel
as he stands
there
in front of a
weeping woman
who sees him not

What shall I now do?
My hands empty
for I have laughed
so long
at their everlasting
defeat all
because of me

Now my lament is deep
for he is alive again
not so much for him
as
for them

What is this haunting
word that
pierces my dark
heart much
as
his hands and feet
were marked?

Its sound frightens me
and now I sense
that
all will be
transformed
This word that changes
everything-
that changes me
Resurrection

DARK FOR THREE DAYS

The light flickered for a
moment in time
only to be extinguished
with the words,
Why have you forsaken me?

And then how dark it was
and a cave of death
sealed up the now
gone light
But the absent light
traveled far and deep
into the darkness
of a cavern
that would be Hell

For a time it seemed
the darkness claimed
victory
But this was no ordinary
light that lost
its radiance
This was the light that
caused suns to blaze
and gave stars their
reason to shine

And so on a day after
a tomorrow that some
thought would never be
the light overcame the darkness
and Resurrection illuminated
the shadow of
death

O indeed it was dark for three days
but never again
will it be
The light of the world
took in the darkness
and sheer love
won

Easter was born in the
very womb of darkness
Still confused disciples
finally saw the
light for
who he was
It took three days
but now
forever has arrived

RUNNING TOWARD RESURRECTION

(The thoughts of Peter and John as they run toward the empty tomb)

I said I loved him . . . but then . . .
And it was I who said *Never*
when the word
denial was uttered
Now we run toward a rumor
of what seems impossible

Empty was his burial
for we were
filled with fear
Some stranger's tomb
is his final home

Why do we run
when we should walk
slowly in our grief?

She said the stone
was rolled away
but that means little
for our faith too
has been removed

Ah yes . . . it is empty
So they have taken him
away . . . again
away from us
but then we deserve
such

Go back we must
but could it be?
We ran toward Resurrection
but we found nothing
But somehow perhaps
he will find us

(Ah the nothing you found
dear disciples
means everything
for soon he will
find you
as today he
finds us
It was and is
Easter
He is risen indeed)

FEEDING TIME

(The thoughts of Simon Peter as Jesus prepares breakfast for him after the Resurrection. John 21:9-19)

Haunting memories of the last
time he broke bread
Now those hands tear
another loaf
but it is my heart
that is broken

I deserve not this meal
nor did I deserve
the last one
It is not the bread
I remember tasting
but my stale words,
I will never deny you

My failure is as hot
as the coals
upon which you now
roast the fish
How can I eat that
which might fill
my stomach
but will never fill
my empty soul?

Eat Simon for you have work
to do
he whispers
But my appetite is gone
after those three
questions about
loving him

I am a crushed rock
that needs to sink
beneath the waves
So I kneel before him
to beg pardon
But he offers not forgiveness
but a command

Now it is you who must
do the feeding
Peter
The past is done
I send you to a
future where
my sheep are hungry

Take this staff and
remember that
you too are a shepherd
Arise now
it is feeding time

A Last Thought

A TRIBUTE TO JIMMY BUFFET

As I close this work and think of the theme of Resurrection, I leave you with my tribute to Jimmy Buffet. I have often used his words in both my writings and even in some sermons. If you are familiar with Jimmy Buffet, you know that many of his words are not suitable for church, but alas, not only was he a wild and crazy guy, he was also a poet who had a great understanding of the human condition.

Jimmy Buffet was one of those figures who got my attention and helped me pause and ponder life and its meaning. Sometimes that pause was to help me and many others celebrate the joy of simply being alive. At other times his words helped me see into life in a deeper way.

This tribute poem ends with Jimmy's own words he wrote near the time of his death knowing that it would be his last song. In this book, I have used Scripture, images from nature, and the seasons of the Christian year to help us all "realize life while we are living it." I now offer you words from a pirate on life's journey who helped this pilgrim Parrot Head pay attention. Sail on Jimmy. Here is my tribute to you as a way to thank you for helping me pay attention:

A PIRATE'S PARADISE

(A tribute to Jimmy Buffet)

So you finally found that
lost shaker of salt
But this time it really was
nobody's fault

It was just past 5 o'clock
somewhere
and you left us parrot heads
sad and unaware

That watch with no numbers
told you the time was "now"
And so you walked off the stage
with just a silent bow

But it is always time
for fruitcakes
with the oven still warm
But the gypsies in the palace
are feeling lost and forlorn

We keep waiting for Monday to
come with that cheeseburger and beer
and it seems Margaritaville
is closed with you not here

Our volcanoes won't blow and
that particular harbor is empty now
Our penciled-in mustaches are faded
in the shadow of a furrowed brow

But then we hear an echo
just beyond a change in latitude
And we hear "fins up"
get a happier attitude

So we check that coconut telegraph
and then we suddenly see
that you're in a pirate's paradise
and not growing older but growing free

So "Bubbles up" all you
seekers of fun and delight
Chew some Juicy Fruit
and remember to smile in the light

For Jimmy, you told us before
and it's true
taste that last mango in Paris
and don't be so blue

So your new paradise watch
is always right
And we will keep on smiling
though you're now out of sight

Your songs live on and continual
joy they will bring
And when we get sad
your last song we will sing:

When your compass is spinnin' and you're lost on the way
Like a leaf in the wind, friend, hear me when I say

Bubbles up, they will point you towards home
No matter how deep or how far you roam
They will show you the surface, the plot and the purpose
So, when the journey gets long, just know that you are loved
There is light up above, and the joy is always enough
Bubbles up

"Bubbles Up." Jimmy Buffet and Will Kimbrough

www.ingramcontent.com/pod-product-compliance
Lightning Source LLC
Chambersburg PA
CBHW050143170426
43197CB00011B/1949